The Journey of Expansion

The Journey of Expansion
A Mothers Journey from Loss to Eternal Love

My Loving Son, Adam

Loretta Holton is the mother of three sons, Adam, Paul, and Daniel. Loretta, as a very young girl, *knew* that she was different. She had strong feelings that there *was* life after death. Her thirst for spiritual knowledge and ancient wisdom became apparent in her teenage years. She began studying on her own, reading, and taking classes with the intention of seeking the greater truth. Loretta always believed in peace and love. Loretta's oldest son, Adam, passed away at the age of seventeen years. Her beliefs in life after death made it easier for her to bear this traumatic loss. Loretta is a natural healer. Her compassionate nature and authentic view on life have led her to the healing field. Loretta is a certified grief and loss facilitator, Reiki master/teacher, angel therapy practitioner, spiritual medium, intuitive, and visionary. Loretta is the author of a line of empathy cards called Messages from Spirit, and she is currently in the process of creating a new line of cards for people who have lost pets. Loretta has received encouragement from many who have read her poems to create this book, which pays tribute to her artistic talent as a poet, writer, and photographer. It is through this medium that Loretta hopes to heal the hearts of many.

The Journey of Expansion
© 2007 by Loretta Holton

www.thejourneyofexpansion.com

ISBN: 978-0-9799478-0-3

Copyediting and layout by Holly Thesieres.
Cover design by Phil Allenbaugh.
Cover photograph by Paul Holton.

Loretta Holton gratefully acknowledges the contributions of Phil Allenbaugh to this volume.

Dedication

I dedicate this book to my three sons, Adam, Paul, and Daniel, who are the greatest blessings and accomplishments in my life. If it were not for Adam's love and devotion to me, this book would not have been possible. His wise and sensitive spirit inherently knew the importance of peace and love. I miss and love you, Adam.

Paul has always been my rock, forever sharing his love, strength, and wisdom. Paul's strong work ethic and sense of responsibility would make any parent proud. I greatly appreciate, more than words can describe, his help with this book and his contribution of the cover photograph, which he took in Hawaii. I am so grateful for and will always cherish the love we have for one another. I love you, Paul.

My youngest son, Daniel, who was extremely close to Adam, suffered major trauma and loss when Adam passed away. Daniel is a very sensitive and creative soul. Adam has given Daniel many signs throughout the years. Time after time, Adam has proven that he is still at Daniel's side. Daniel's fun-loving spirit and compassionate nature have shown me that his loyalty, love, and support are always there, regardless of the situation. Daniel was my gift, and I am grateful for the deep love we share. I love you, Daniel.

My strongest hope and desire is to instill the belief that anyone who wants to make contact with his or her deceased loved one can. It is possible! Be open to believing, and whenever you think or feel that you may have received a sign, you most likely have. Trust yourself.

Gratitude

To my mother, Mary Ann Cristando, and my brother John Cristando Jr., who are both in Spirit. You have both been a true inspiration to me, allowing me to be blessed with your eternal love and presence. I have learned so much from both of you. You have remained a constant source of encouragement. Words cannot describe how much I miss each of you.

To my father, John Cristando Sr.—thank you, Dad, so much for your words of love and wisdom. Also, thank you for your financial support during this self-evolving process. Your belief in me has meant everything. I love you so much.

To my brother Thomas Cristando—my deepest love and gratitude goes out to you for everything we have been through in our lives. Our love and friendship are so strong that I am forever grateful.

To my beloved soul mate, David Wilson, who is the man of my dreams. I am so grateful for your love, devotion, and loyalty. Thank you for all your support. You have always listened to me when I spoke my truth! I know that Adam brought us together because it was our destiny. I love you!

To my son's father, Alex J. Holton, for giving me the three most loving, sensitive, and nurturing boys a mother could ever want. I am so thankful for your ever-inspiring encouragement and our long and continued friendship.

To my oldest and best friend, Josie Stoneking, who has been my shining star. For the past ten years, since Adam's death, I know that I could not have made it without you. I know Adam brought us together because without your loyalty, devotion, encouragement, and love, this book would not have been possible. I am forever grateful for our love and sacred friendship.

To one of my closest friends, Lisa McMillan, who is such an intuitive and sensitive soul. You have always been there for me. You have given me the most profound messages from Adam. Additionally, thank you for helping me to sell my line of cards and for your support with not only this book, but my life. You have been a loyal and true friend. You have my deepest respect, love, and gratitude.

To my soul sister, Vicki Cobb-Jenkins—words cannot express how I feel about you. Our hearts connect us. I am so grateful you are in my life. Thank you for helping me edit my book and for your positive input. I love you.

To Dr. Jane San Juan, a close and dear friend, who has had a major impact on my life. I appreciate all the questions you have asked me about my book. Your questions have helped me to enhance my thought process and stay on target.

To my teacher Diana Wint—thank you for all your love and encouraging words throughout our friendship. The mediumship class I took from you gave me the confidence in myself to enhance my abilities. You have empowered me to move forward with my work as a writer, healer, and visionary, but most of all, you have taught me the ability to trust my truth and myself.

To all my sisters in the circle who have given me such awesome readings and who have encouraged me to hold on to my dreams and my heart's desire—thank you Vicki Cobb-Jenkins, Frances Greenspan, Heather Heintz, Rita Hopkins, Mary Ann Loconte, Meg Tweedy, Diana Wint, and Terry Zeschmann. You all have your own unique gifts and talents that need to be shared with the world.

To Dr. James Martin Peebles, who died in 1922 at almost one hundred years of age and who is channeled through Trance Medium Summer Bacon. It was Dr. Peeble's unconditional words of love, insight, and wisdom that helped me to transform my life into one of greater truth and awareness. When I first spoke with you, Dr. Peebles, you mentioned that I would be writing a book, and you gave me the title of my book—so here it is! I am eternally grateful to you for letting me know that I am deeply loved and for helping me to lighten up just a little bit. God bless you indeed.

Table of Contents

ONE

∞

Introduction

When Adam was sixteen years old, he said, "If I should die young, Mom, please don't be sad; be happy because I am going to live my life to its fullest."

"Mom, if I should die young, please don't be sad; be happy because I am going to live my life to its fullest."

Adam's comment astounded me. I looked at him and gasped. Tears immediately began to flow. I replied, "If you do, will you come back to visit me?"

He replied, "Of course I will, Mom."

These were the words spoken by my son Adam just months before his death. Adam must have known on a soul level that he was going to leave this earthly plane.

Since his transition to the spirit world, Adam has kept his promise. His spirit is always around me as he continues to give me signs on a daily basis.

In the spring of 1997, I experienced the greatest heartbreak a parent can imagine. At only seventeen years of age, my oldest son, Adam, fell tragically to his death while doing something he loved to do: rock climbing with his friends in Lake Tahoe, Nevada.

After experiencing this tremendous loss, I was left to reexamine my views on God, life, and what follows our existence on Earth. I needed to understand what happened and why. In my desperation to find answers and attempt to deal with my extreme feelings of grief, I began to examine ways in which to channel the intense feelings as well as search for truth and meaning. During my search for further clarity, I researched many different avenues. I spent countless hours with Adam's friends discussing past experiences. I desperately wanted to be part of their lives because they had been such an important part of Adam's life. I felt that being close to them would somehow make me feel closer to Adam.

I held an informal memorial with Adam's friends at one of his favorite places overlooking Lake Michigan. It was a place where Adam's friends felt free to express their deepest feelings, to watch the sunset, and to enjoy each other's company. We sang songs and exchanged fellowship. We planted a pine tree and placed a commemorative plaque in the ground to serve as a living memorial to Adam. As the sun set, I felt Adam's presence around us.

Spending time with friends and family helped a great deal, but it was still not enough. I needed to understand Adam's unexpected passing. I began to read books and to research any material that I could find about spirituality and life-after-death experiences. I fully wanted to understand what happens after we leave this world. I always had a strong belief in life after death. It was comforting to know how many books had been written on the subject and how many others had encountered this type of experience. The validation of these occurrences reinforced both my thoughts and my feelings.

Despite all my questions and overwhelming sadness, I made a decision to move on. It was important to make life as normal as possible for the sake of my remaining two sons. My middle son, Paul, was fourteen years old, and my youngest son, Daniel, was just five years old. Most important, I knew that to enable my family to move on with their lives, I had to heal and move on with mine. Because of a strong will and trust in God, I was able to pass through the traumatic difficulties that had become an intrinsic part of my existence.

Out of all the people affected by the loss of Adam, I thought my mother would be the most understanding of my need for love and support. Interestingly, she was the least. Adam was staying with my mother at the time just prior to his death. The morning that Adam left to go rock climbing was the last time my mother saw him alive. He kissed her on the back of her neck and said, "You're the best, Grandma. I love you."

When my mother shared his final words with me, I could feel her pain and tremendous grief and sorrow. It was also clear that she felt responsible for Adam's death. Weeks would go by without hearing a word from her. When she would call, she never inquired about my feelings or the pain that I was experiencing. Adam was her first grandchild, and they were inseparable. Initially, I felt abandoned that my mother could not offer me compassion or console me. As a daughter, I just wanted my mother. I felt very alone. In retrospect, it is easier to understand now how my mother was so depressed by Adam's death that she, too, was emotionally unavailable to anyone else. Who can measure the depth of someone else's pain or the ability to cope with such a staggering loss?

My mother moved to Oregon soon after Adam passed away and died about four years later. My younger brother Tom, my nephew Ryan, and I went to her home to pack up her belongings. Although my mother and I would talk on the phone, I had not seen her since Adam had fallen to his death. As soon as we walked into her kitchen, I looked up, and there was Adam's senior high school picture sitting on the shelf directly above the sink. I immediately started to cry. She had kept Adam center stage in her heart. I could picture my mother talking to Adam every day as she did her dishes. It was at this moment that I felt my mother's deep feelings of sadness and realized that she had never reconciled herself to Adam's death. She had kept all her feelings to herself. It was also at this time that I was able to look at the nature of grief, and I recognized that it is such a personal and selfish thing—it is difficult to imagine anyone else experiencing the same kind of pain that you are experiencing.

Barbie, my sister-in-law, provided me with the support that my mother was unable to give and that I was unable to give my mother. This is not an uncommon situation—oftentimes, good friends, outside family members, or other unexpected people are able to give more support since they are not directly involved. Or perhaps it could be their compassionate and understanding nature.

Barbie lived halfway across the country, but she called me continuously and would send angel cards to me on a regular basis. Her kind gestures made me aware of how much she loved me and that she was thinking of me. I found that having someone listen to me and caring enough to call was all I needed. The ultimate loss changed our lives forever. Our perspective about life and people will never be the same again.

After Adam passed away, he would give messages to his Aunt Barbie in her dreams. He would show her pictures in her dreams of me sobbing uncontrollably and overwhelmed with grief. After receiving these messages from Adam, Barbie would call me and ask me how I was doing. I would tell her that I was not doing very well. This happened on several occasions.

I remember Barbie telling me about the very first visitation that Adam paid her. Barbie saw herself in the dream. Adam was surrounded by white light, and his face was iridescent and glowing. He was wearing his favorite blue sweatshirt, which I believe was a frame of reference. Adam wanted us to know it was more than a dream. Adam took Barbie's hand and said, "Follow me."

The dream scene took place in a house; Adam was leading his aunt from room to room, searching for me. They discovered me in an all-white kitchen, looking out the window and talking on an old telephone with a red cord. I was dressed all in white, except for a rose-colored shirt, which symbolically stands for love. I was surrounded by white light. I was crying hysterically on the phone. Adam wanted Barbie to understand how upset I was. Adam grabbed Barbie's hand once again, and they left the room. She kissed Adam good-bye, and then Barbie woke up crying. She was upset because the dream had felt so real. Adam knew that Barbie was receptive to psychic impressions and that she was a gifted medium. Minutes after the dream, she called to share Adam's visit with me. The timing could not have been more perfect. I had been crying, and I was feeling very alone.

Adam, at this time, was unable to make contact with me directly because I was consumed with deep sorrow. It not only helped me, but it also helped Barbie's grieving process and healing as well.

I will always be grateful for Barbie's constant love and support. I could not have gone through this process without her. The remarkable thing was that these visitations further substantiated the fact that my son was living up to his promise. He was coming back to visit me in any way possible.

Counseling became a natural and important part of my grieving process. I had a great spiritual connection with my counselor—so much so that I have become a certified grief and loss facilitator working with childhood loss and family bereavement. The greatest healing asset and benefit for me is the ability to comfort others in the time of their grief and loss.

One of my counselor's suggestions was to capture my feelings and emotions on paper. I am glad I did. If I had not written anything down, I never would have remembered the emotional gambit that I experienced: dreams I may have had; how my children were dealing with their own grief and loss; how I was feeling—love, joy, sadness, laughter, and tears; and how much I missed Adam. I was amazed how much I had forgotten during that time in my life. The saying that you will feel numb is so true.

My counselor's suggestion led me to the idea of starting a journal not just for me, but also for Daniel and for Adam's close friends and family as well. It was my hope that the journal would document Adam's life, relationships, and experiences as seen through his friends' and family's eyes and hearts. When completed, the journal was intended to be a living testimony to Adam's short life and the dynamic impact that he had on others. We all make a difference. Ultimately, the journal will be passed on to Daniel, Adam's youngest brother. Daniel followed Adam everywhere. Adam loved to play with Daniel and assumed the role of Daniel's protector. This journal will provide an ongoing connection to Adam and serve as a written memory for Daniel to treasure for the rest of his life.

The response to the journal from our family and friends was astounding. Everyone close to Adam was eager to share his or her feelings and speak to Adam through this type of medium. However, it took months before Adam's father, Alex, and his middle brother, Paul, could express themselves in this form. It was seven months before Paul picked up the journal and took it up to his room to read what others had said about his brother. Finally, Paul came down the stairs hours later and placed the journal directly in front of me. He was finally able to express his thoughts and pent-up grief regarding his brother's passing. I opened the journal to read what Paul had written and immediately started to cry. I cried so hard that the words on the page began to blur. This single act signified a tremendous release and expansive emotional healing for Paul.

It also took several months for some of Adam's friends to write in the journal. Adam's passing devastated his entire circle of friends. They were all very close. To see Adam's friends, to listen to them, and to read what they wrote in the journal about their own feelings of pain, loss, and love for Adam was overwhelming. What I discovered was that as much as I wanted to see his friends, they were a realistic reminder that they were all alive and that I would never see my son again.

Our family was living in Michigan when Adam died in May 1997. Alex, Adam's father, received a job transfer. Nine months later, we returned to California, where we were originally from. Under the circumstances, we were happy to leave Michigan. However, I wanted to get Adam's friends together one last time to say my good-byes. I felt that I would never see them again.

I spoke to Josh, Adam's best friend, and asked him to invite Adam's friends for a specific date. Whoever showed up was meant to be there. To my delight, they all came. I had been so close to them that most of them called me Mom.

Keith, one of Adam's close and longtime friends, was the only one of Adam's friends that I had not seen since Adam died. Nearly nine months had passed. That night, there was a knock on the door. When I opened it, Keith just stood there. He was still overcome with grief and sadness. We just hugged each other. Keith was the only one that had not yet written in the journal. I handed the journal to Keith and asked him if he would write something to Adam. Keith picked up the pen and, with a deep sigh, wrote a short note on the bottom right-hand corner of one of the pages. It stated, "Adam, [I am] going to keep it together. Keith."

My first thought was, *Is that all he is going to write?*

However, in his deep despair, that was all he could write. Although short, it was very profound. Keith was overwhelmed. He did not know how to express his grief.

From the early entries in the journal, the powerful and compelling impact Adam had on others' lives became quite clear to me. It gave me solace knowing that so many loved him and respected him as their best friend. This journal had become a tool to heal not only my heart and soul, but those of all who loved him.

Since the time of Adam's passing, I have become extremely aware of children who have had to go through major trauma and loss. Often, children are not allowed to grieve properly. Both adults and children need to receive counseling, either in a support group or by discussing and sharing their deepest feelings of sadness, anger, and blame with a knowledgeable adult. Counseling is critical. It is important that children be allowed to grieve in a positive and healing environment or to solicit a professional to encourage them to express their most profound emotions and feelings. If not, it will affect their ability to cope with relationships for the rest of their lives. I have listened to many people in the various groups that I have attended, who come from all lifestyles. All of them have experienced problems with coping and relationship skills.

One grown man, in his thirties, mentioned that he had lost his best friend in high school from a motorcycle accident. He had cried at home, and his father had said, "If you are going to cry, then go to your room and shut the door."

The statement not only lacked compassion, but also, it relayed the message that it is wrong to feel or to have emotions. This message negates the very essence of our souls. Life is about feelings and finding the balance between the head and the heart. If we repress our feelings, we repress our hearts.

The moment I received the phone call from my mother about Adam's death, I was in total shock and disbelief. We all were. I am so glad that Alex was there because he took care of everything—all the arrangements. My two other sons clung to me. Paul, my middle son, began to tremble and shake, and Daniel, my youngest son, began to weep. Suddenly, I heard Adam's voice: "Mom, I am right here and I am fine. But you need to go on, not only for yourself, but for my brothers."

I decided immediately that my two children needed my love and support more than ever. Adam's statement did not surprise me for he always looked out for his brothers, and he still does, working from the other side. As difficult as it was at times, we managed to get through the worst part of the grieving process the best that we could. Emotions still arise today, and sometimes it requires additional counseling. It has become easier, but you never forget.

Two weeks after Adam passed, Paul and Daniel had baseball games scheduled to play at the same time. The fields were next to each other. Alex and I made a decision to attend both games individually to keep our sons' lives as normal as possible. It was difficult because it was the first time I had been in public. I felt very self-conscious and that everyone was looking at us. In retrospect, I know now that everyone was feeling such a sense of compassion for our family. One of the mothers came up to us and expressed her condolences to Alex and me. She had three children of her own. She looked directly into my eyes and said, "I don't know how you can do it. I would be curled up in a corner and would never want to leave."

I responded, "I felt that I had to think about my other two children and the impact that Adam's death has had on their lives."

All parents who have gone through losing a child know exactly how it feels, and yet everyone deals with it differently. All of us have learned different coping skills, and all of us are unique. Without a doubt, this is a parent's worst nightmare. As adults, it is difficult to cope with our own traumas, grief, and losses, but for the children left behind, it can be twice as devastating for they have not yet experienced tragedy in their lives, nor do they know how to handle it. Often, they are overshadowed by the deceased member of the family and become ignored. I have met parents who have become so consumed with grief that they completely forgot about the rest of their family. Years go by, and the parent is still stuck in the anger stage of grief. I cannot stress enough the importance of seeking guidance for the entire family.

While attending my bereavement classes, I was amazed at the number of trite clichés there are about grieving. For example, according to Reverend Alice Parsons Zulli in her book *Beyond Loss*,[1] people sometimes offer condolences that they assume are comforting and soothing but prove to be just the opposite, for example, *it was God?s will*; *you have other children*; *God never gives you more than you can handle*; *it was for the best*; *you just need a little time*.

It is important to recognize the naïveté with which people handle their condolences. They mean well, but the above statements are not well received by the grieving person. Per Reverend Zulli, to state that you just need a little more time is insensitive. The grieving person is having difficulty just getting through a single day.

It was for the best or *he is better off* are others that are inappropriate. If the grieving person has watched his or her loved one suffer with physical or psychological pain, he or she may come to this conclusion for himself or herself. It is not up to us to decide when he or she should be reconciled to this fact and whether or not it is for the best. Whose best? The grieving person left behind is not always better off. The solution is simple: be compassionate, be patient, and just listen. Listening with your heart is often all the grieving person needs. Do not say something just because you are at a loss for words. Share your love and empathy, and let the grieving person know you are always there if he or she needs to talk.

Most of us choose not to discuss death, and yet we all die. As difficult as it is on this physical plane to understand its meaning, our loved ones who are crossed over want us to move on with our lives. They want us to celebrate their love and the life that was shared with them. You would not feel the grief and the sadness if the love that you shared were not so deeply connected. Each relationship that we have while on the earthly plane is for a reason. Each of us has been brought together to dispel Karma and learn specific lessons. You may rejoice in the fact that you and your loved one will be together again. He or she, too, has a destination. He or she continues to grow and learn even after death. Soul evolution is important on both sides of the veil.

I chose to deal with my son's death the only way I knew how: I wanted my other sons, Paul and Daniel, to be able to grieve for Adam, their brother, in the healthiest, most positive and loving way possible. His brothers and I still talk about Adam a lot. He will always remain in our hearts.

If you know a child that needs attention regarding grief, trauma, or loss, please do your best to reach out to the child or his or her parents. Take action. If you do not feel that you can discuss the topic with the child, then give him or her a copy of this book. I am sure that he or she will eventually be very grateful.

Since Adam's transition to the spirit world, Adam has kept his promise. I have been very blessed in knowing that his sprit is always around me as he continues to give me signs on a daily basis. The experience of knowing and loving my first son, Adam, and understanding his death has made me a stronger, better, and more evolved person. I continue to grow even after his passing. Adam's strong and powerful spirit has given me the courage and strength to write the inspirational poems found in chapter 3 of this book as channeled through the words of a seventeen-year-old young man: poems that I pray will give hope to others—hope combined with the fundamental faith that life really does go on in the spiritual realm, as our lives here on Earth must go on.

Note

1.   Alice Parsons Zulli, *Beyond Loss* (Pine Mountain, CA, 1997).

TWO

∞

How the Messages Began

"The more we heal in physicality, the more we acknowledge our loved ones' presence and the more our loved ones will demonstrate that there is an afterlife."

It was two years after Adam's passing when I became inspired to write. I sat down with pen in hand, and the words just began to flow. The title of the poem came first. Once the title was written down, the words became messages, and the process became real. The messages would come in clusters. Then they would stop as quickly as they came. I would try to force the process, but nothing would happen. Then, suddenly, a title would come to mind, and the words would follow. There were times I would be in the shower and suddenly become inspired—I would jump out of the shower and begin to write. Water is a conduit to Spirit. I have met several people who have gotten a lot of information while in the shower. The water attracts your angels, too.

I would also receive inspiration while driving in my car. I would stop the car, grab a piece of paper, and begin to write, and again, the words would follow.

After writing several of these poems, I decided to share them with family and friends. As others would read the poems, they would cry, and all would comment on how beautiful and healing they were. Some would say that I should consolidate all of them and write a book. Others would say they would make great cards! When someone I knew lost a loved one, I would copy one of my poems that I felt was appropriate to his or her loved one's passing and give it to the person, who I felt needed to hear the message. The response was always overwhelming. I *knew* in my heart and soul that I was being blessed with Divine Intervention. From the beginning, I felt the messages were emerging from my son Adam.

I visited a world-renowned medium who was visiting in my area. All the questions I had about Adam were validated. When I asked about the writings, the medium just laughed and said, "Of course they are coming from Adam. Where else did you think they were coming from?"

All of my close friends and family validated this because they knew how close the spiritual connection was between Adam and me. I was on a mission.

Throughout the past several years, I have written more than sixty poems that have helped heal my spirit in countless ways. In addition to the line of greeting cards that I produced, many said I needed to incorporate my poetry into a book to help heal the hearts of many. I have taken pictures of sunsets for years where I live. My vision to match the poems to specific sunsets was born, and thus this book finally came together.

Our loved ones on the other side want us to know that there is no death. It is only a transition from the physical body to the spiritual body. We return home. The more we heal in physicality, the more we acknowledge our loved ones' presence and the more our loved ones will demonstrate that there is an afterlife. We just need to be open to receiving them. Our loved ones do not stop growing just because they have passed on. They continue to grow, as we continue to grow. We help each other. Adam always reminds me of this. Every time I have asked him to give me a sign, he has always followed through—oftentimes in subtle ways, and oftentimes in vast ways.

I hope you can become inspired through these profound and beautiful messages as you grow and progress on your path, always knowing that *Love Is Eternal and Never Dies.*

THREE

∞

Poetry or Messages from Adam

"I hope and pray that you can see that death is not a final destiny."

Released

My body was tired
and in a lot of pain.
Now my spirit is
free and young again.

Thank you so much
for taking care of me.
You were the best
anyone could be.

You showed me so much
love, compassion and giving.
That is what made me want
to go on living.

Life is not over when you die.
There are never any
real good-byes.

I love you.

"Released" has had an impact on so many people who have read, received, or bought this card for someone they love. Many have shared their stories with me about how Adam's beautiful message has touched theirs or a loved one's heart. They have immediately started to cry! They often state that it is such a powerful and healing card.

Celebrate

Celebrate the loss of a loved one.
What a wonderful gift to be able
to look back on the love, peace and
kindness that your loved one came to give.

If you look at life as a play
and we all play a part,
we all have special gifts and talents.
Some of us know from the start.

Celebrate the loss of a loved one,
rather than feeling sad,
for our life is but a journey
and your loved one will be glad.

Life is a precious gift
that we all need to treasure.
For in a moment's time
your life can change forever.

Just keep in your mind when
it is your time to go, people
will celebrate your life.
You will see that we live
and love for eternity.

As humans, it is important and natural to grieve. In other countries, it is very natural to celebrate loss. No matter what you believe and when you are ready, there is always a precious gift that your loved one has left and given you. The most beautiful gift we can give ourselves is to celebrate our loved one's love and loss. The only thing that is real is love! An older woman lost her husband of fifty-six years. She was in deep grief and sorrow. She had lost her best friend. She could not move past the hurt and pain. Her granddaughter purchased the card "Celebrate" and gave it to her. When she received the card, she started to cry. Her granddaughter said, "Read the back of the card," which relayed my journey with Adam. The grandmother related so profoundly that she felt it was a message from her husband. The grandmother placed the card on her refrigerator to read every day!

Live Life

Do not take life for granted,
for it is not for you to see
when we must leave this plane
in order to be free.

You must live life to the fullest.
Even though I am not there.
I will never be far from you
if you fall into despair.

Do not ever forget—
I am not far away.
I am here on the other side
enjoying the stay.

I am very happy here.
So please understand
when your time comes,
I will give you my hand.
I will help you cross over to
the promised land.

The last time I saw Adam alive, he hugged me so tightly that I thought it was incredibly intense. We both said I love you. As I look back, his soul knew. We must always show and express our love to one another for we never know how long we may have. Adam had a very tumultuous relationship with his grandfather, but the last thing he said to his grandfather was I love you. The more people talk about when their loved ones pass away, the more I am convinced that the soul knows when it is ready to leave this plane. Even when I got together with Adam's friends, a few of them shared their stories about what Adam had relayed about some of the unfinished situations that he felt needed to be healed. It taught me always to say I love you to the people I care about and never leave anything incomplete.

Forgive Me

I'm sorry I took my life so soon.
I could not help it
for I was in such deep gloom.

I was so wrong I'm sorry to say,
I never meant to hurt you in this way.

Please pray for me and always send me love.
It will help me to grow in spirit,
reinforcing peace from above.

Never give up hope and continue to pray
for my spirit will illuminate in its own unique way.

Spiritual guides are helping me heal into the light,
so please have faith. Do not lose sight.

I am so sorry, so sorry you see—
I never meant to hurt you,

so please forgive me!

When Adam was a younger teenager, he experienced some deep depression. He talked about killing himself. He felt tremendous loss when we moved our family from California to Michigan. Alex, my son's father, and I placed him into counseling immediately. Adam now works with adolescents on the spiritual plane as well as on the earthly plane who are contemplating suicide or who have already experienced suicide. This statement has been validated by many psychic and medium friends.

Blame

Please don't blame God.
It was my time to go.
It was a choice I made
a long time ago.

I had a great life
during my stay.
You taught me how to love
and be kind in my own way.

Be open to the awareness
that I am close by.
I'll be there if you need me
in a blink of an eye.

I carry your love for me
deep within my soul.
If you feel the need to cry,
I'm always close by . . .

Just let it go!

The first time I had my empathy cards displayed, a mother picked up this particular card and immediately bought it from me. Her twenty-nine-year-old son had died in a car accident. He had been drinking, and she blamed herself. If you continue to hold on to blame, it will hold you back from the healing process. Your loved one on the other side is trying to get your attention to let you know that it was his or her time and not to blame yourself.

Anger

Please don't be angry
and never ask why.
It was my time to go.
We never say good-bye.

Death is but a transition;
it is never final.
Get on with your life,
and don't live in denial.

I know you miss me
and love me so.
But you must move on.
You must let me go.

I will pray for peace
to enter your soul,
and always remember,

I Love You!

Anger is a natural part of the grieving process. Any emotion or feeling is normal as long as it does not hold you back from moving forward after a period of time. I did not experience much anger because I knew that on a deeper level, it was meant to be. I also knew I had to go on for my two other sons, who needed me and who were still on the earthly plane. Some people stay angry for years instead of accepting the loss. This emotion keeps both the departed loved one and the parent, relative, or friend from evolving. Let God! Let go!

Sorrow

I know you're in such deep pain and sorrow.
There is always a new tomorrow.

I hope and pray that you can see
that death is not a final destiny.

I used to think that when I was on Earth,
but now that I'm here, I know the truth.

It is just a transition, without fear or strife.
Once you understand, you can live your life.

Live with kindness, compassion and love.
All the answers will come from above.

Look deep in your heart, and then you will see
the beautiful being you were meant to be.

Please know that I love you with all my heart
and always know that we will never part.

When we grieve and feel sorrow, it is as though we are stuck. It hurts so much. Finding someone to talk to is important. As you speak about your loved one, it brings out all those feelings and emotions that need to be expressed. If you hold on to them, it will create pain, and the emotions will manifest in the physical body. Move forward!

I Am So Happy

I know your heart is hurting.
It was my time to go.
Now it's time for healing.
I'll help you to grow.

Oh, it's so beautiful here—
I wish you could see
I am so happy,
as happy as I can be.

I know it's hard
for you to understand.
In time, I know,
you shall need my hand.

When you open your heart
to the spiritual realm,
I will let you know
that I am always around.

When our loved ones cross over, they immediately feel a complete release from their bodies. Their spirits are set free. Most try immediately to make contact with us, but we are usually so grief stricken that we lose the opportunity. There are people who see, hear, or feel Spirit, or just know that Spirit is around. These people are the ones who are open to Spirit and who have been so since birth. There are others yet who have developed the gift through education or through the passing of a loved one. Try to have faith and be open to the contact.

Soul's Journey

I am on my soul's journey,
so don't be afraid.
I will be with you always.
I will come to you in visions and
dreams and in subtle ways.
Through words, in songs, and books,
through rivers and streams,
through sunsets and sunrises,
and flowers and moonbeams,
I will be with you always.

Through the years, Adam has come to me in numerous ways. I have experienced him in all of the above ways and more. He has paid me many visitations in my dreams. The first visitation Adam made was to his brother Paul. It was profound. One night, he called me on the phone, and we had a special conversation (see chapter 4).

Joined by the Heart

Your heart is hurting.
You feel so numb.
The painful journey
has just begun.

The one you love
is so very near
for the love you have
you hold so dear.

Love is eternal.
You're joined by the heart.
Just be open to new beginnings
for we will never part.

Open your eyes
for love never dies.

I received more than one hundred sixty cards when Adam passed away. There were so many people expressing their heartfelt sympathy, not knowing what to say other than that they were sorry for our loss. The two cards that stood out were from parents that had lost a child, who said, "We know how you feel. It will take about six months until the numbness wears off." If I had not written everything down during that time in my life, I would not have remembered anything. The love I have for Adam is so strong that I was able to get through it, no matter how difficult it was.

No Accidents

There are no accidents;
it was my time.
Believe in this
and in the Divine.

My time was short lived.
But while I was there,
I learned many lessons—
how to love and to share.

The greatest gift of all
is the gift of love
for this comes
from above.

My lessons were learned,
it was my time to go.
I'm always with you.
I love you so.

When Adam fell to his death, I really felt that it was not an accident. I felt that it was meant to be. It was his time. One of the girls Adam was with felt responsible because it was her idea to go to the rock from which Adam fell. I said to her that Adam made a choice. She did not need to place that kind of guilt or blame on herself. It was enough that she was going to have to live with the trauma of experiencing the death of my son. I believe we all make choices, and even when we do not choose, we still make a choice not to choose. I believe on some level that our souls have windows or exit points through which we choose to leave the earthly plane.

A Mother and Son

I know you miss me deeply and you love me so.
I can see your heart is hurting for I can feel your soul.

It's been a while since you've seen me,
but I've never left your side.
I have been with you always, morning, noon and night.

As I am brushing your tears from your face,
you are being filled with God's compassion and loving Grace.

There are no accidents, Mom; it was my time to go.
It's hard to understand, but you really must know.

You are such a great mom; I just want you to know,
we will always be connected. I do love you so.

Please get on with your journey so I can continue mine.
I love you, Mom, and I always will, until the end of time.

My best friend asked me to write a poem for her friend who had lost her young son through a train incident. The mother was having tremendous difficulty with the loss. I sat down, and the words started to flow. As I was writing, tears began to flow. I knew Adam was coming through to give me this inspiring message. It gave me such tremendous healing.

Stillborn

I know you were awaiting my arrival,
but it was not meant to be.
It was already planned eons ago.
It was our destiny.
It was just enough time for me to feel your love.
Before I returned to the heavens above.

I know your heart is hurting and it's hard for you to move on.
Always remember my love for you is always so strong.
You blame yourself, but please understand it was my time.
We will always be connected to the Divine.

We have been together before, and we will be together again
embraced in God's loving arms—where it all began.
When you feel the need to cry, I will be by your side
loving and supporting you, and to be your guide.

I know how much you love me.
You will always wonder why.
It was just meant to be.
There are never any good-byes.
I love you, Mommy.
Love is eternal and never dies.

My older sister Lenora was stillborn, and my mother mourned her for years. I did not understand the depth of pain my mother went through until my own son Adam passed away. When I was younger, we would visit Lenora's grave site on special occasions. This poem was a message from Adam to help better understand my relationship with my mother and her grieving process. It does not matter how young or old our children are; they will remain in our hearts forever.

Tears

I wish I could wipe the tears from your face
and fill you with God's loving grace.

Every tear is a prayer, a prayer from you to me.
Oh, how I wish you could see
how happy I am and free.

I wish you could see how beautiful
and peaceful it is as I look down upon you.
I'm sending you love and light.
If only you could share my vision and my sight—

The sight of beauty everywhere you go
is the essence of love and how the spirits glow.

Life is sacred; you must move on and be free.
I'll always be close by to give you what
you always gave to me—

Love.

Tears are as natural as the sunshine. Tears are cleansing as well as healing. They are a part of the natural grieving process. I can remember many times when they would flow uncontrollably. I would hear Adam say, "I'm right here!" It does not stop the feeling of wanting to see your loved one. Tears truly are a prayer between you and your loved one. They are also a release. Cry!

The Dream

I came to you last night in a dream
just to let you know that everything is
great and I love you so.
Please don't worry about me.
I have been set free;
I am as happy as I can be.

I know I've reached a level
that you do not quite understand.
If and when you are ready
I will take you by the hand.
We will fly away to the
beauty of this Promised Land.

I know the dream was short and sweet,
but the message was loud and clear—
how much I love you, Mommy,
and I am *always* near.

Just be open to the awareness
there is more to life than this.
Soon, I will take you on a journey
into this heavenly bliss.

Adam has paid me many visitations throughout the years. I can remember them as if they were yesterday. The difference between a visit and a dream is that a dream can be a bit foggy. You do not remember a dream clearly, but a visitation is very clear. Adam always had so much love for me, either by telling me he loved me or by just hugging me tightly. I cherish those memories for they were and always will be very sacred to me.

Heaven

Butterflies are a symbol of transformation and rebirth.
This is what happened to me when I left the earth.
When I came to the light, I was overwhelmed with love.
I knew then I was in God's holy heaven above.

Friends and family came to greet me at this time.
They were so full of love and were able to feel
my heart and to read my mind.
I was free of my body but it felt so at home.
It felt so familiar. I just wanted to roam.

They showed me all the beautiful mountains and streams,
flowers, rainbows, colors and spiritual beings.
There were children and animals playing all around.
There was so much love to be found.
Please do not be sad; just be at peace and go your way.
When it's your time, I will be there to greet you
on your chosen day.

When we leave this plane, we go exactly where we think or believe we will go. We create whatever we need to make us feel comfortable on the other side. We will take our consciousnesses and souls with us. If our belief is to go to the light, our family and friends will be there to greet us. It is such a beautiful, holy, and loving energy. If we believe in hell (lower dimension), then we will create hell. If we believe in heaven (higher dimension), we will create heaven. We are the soul creators of our own reality on either side of the veil.

It Seems Impossible

Laughter and joy seem so impossible when
someone you love passes away
for at the time it happens, it feels as though
you cannot make it through another day.
Even though your life will never be the same again,
I hope that someday you will find joy and laughter
in your own time and in your own way.

When someone you love makes the transition,
they just want you to know
that they are safe and happy and
how much they love you so.
When you can begin to laugh again and
feel joy in your soul, it is such a blessing that
you cannot help but grow.

You see, they never stop thinking of you
even though they are not in your sight.
When you begin to heal and find peace in your heart,
then the impossible seems so right!

It seemed impossible to laugh and feel any kind of joy for quite some time. I kept to myself and with my immediate family, which made me feel safe. In a month's time, I returned to work, but it was difficult to be around people who did not understand my loss. I did not want to discuss my grief as it became more difficult and it made me feel worse. It made me feel guilty to think about any kind of joy or happiness. After all, how could I feel happy when my son just died? Eventually, as I began to feel Adam's presence and love for me, I allowed myself to experience joy and laughter once again.

Feeling the Loss

When you lose someone you love,
you are in such deep grief and sorrow,
you honestly feel you will not see tomorrow.

Your body becomes numb.
All you can feel is the pain.
Accept there is nothing that you can change.

Your heart has been torn out—
a feeling that you cannot describe.
You feel so hopeless that you want to die.

Every tear that you cry is sacred.
Only your loved one can hear.
Each one is a prayer that God is near.

After a while, with God's loving grace,
you will feel the love and warm embrace.
Feel secure that your loved one is near,
sending you a message loud and clear.

They want you to know they are happy and free,
right where they are meant to be
to fulfill their destiny.

Their love for you is eternal—it will never die.
So when you feel helpless and you just sigh,
look up to heaven and know they are close by.

Just hold on to this thought—
you will be together someday.
They will be there to show you the way.

This message expresses exactly how I felt and still feel. Adam's message is not only for me, but also for others as well to let all know that your loved ones never leave your side.

Holiday Season

The holiday season is a special time when your
families are near; but for those who have
lost loved ones, it is a sad time of year.

In the silence of the night, you wonder what it
would be like again to hold your loved one
in your arms and to look back when it all began.

You remember the precious memories of times past.
It seems like it was only yesterday.
Yet there are memories that seem so distant, so far away.

As you reflect upon this holiday season,
the spirit of love and light,
it helps you to cherish the ones you love who
are with God and angels who look upon us
and shine so bright.

Even though we miss them and love them so,
let us rejoice in their spirits at this holy time,
always to remember we are one
and connected to the Divine.

Holidays always bring up feelings of sadness and loss. Whether it is a Thanksgiving surrounded by family and friends, or Christmastime tree-trimming with ornaments that our loved ones made, it is necessary to move on and create new memories—for this is what our loved ones want us to do. Remember them, cherish their memories, and always carry them in your heart. They will never die.

First-Year Anniversary

It has been nearly a year since the day I passed away.
I can feel you are overwhelmed with grief as you try to
remember every step we made together—to reconstruct
the moment your life changed forever.

You know that you cannot change what happened to me.
If you can comprehend what I am about to say,
it was meant for me to go this way.

As my spirit left my body, I was guided to the light.
It felt so peaceful, warm, and loving.
It seemed so right.

As I reflect back on the past, it was clear to see
that everything happened for a reason,
and you were the best anyone could ever be.

I visit you quite often, giving you light and love
hoping that someday soon
you can move on with your life.

When the day comes when you are ready,
I will be ready, too, to continue on our spiritual
journey, just like we are supposed to do.

You will always have the memories and pictures
to reflect on the past, but the love that is
within our hearts will forever last.

The first anniversary is extremely difficult. As the date approaches, your emotions will accelerate. Whenever I meet someone who has not been through it, I let him or her know that this is natural and that it is part of the process of grief and loss.

Time to Move On

When you know it is time to move on,
surrender to the new dawn.

Listen to your heart: let it be your guide.
Speak the truth, and do not hide.

Trust in Spirit to show you the way
in order to make it through another day.

The time together was meant to be.
As you reflect, you can see

lessons learned; it is time to let go.
Break free—go with the flow.

There are never any mistakes, so learn
from the past.
Love is eternal and will forever last.

Thank you so much for loving me.
My spirit has been set free!

I release you...

When we hold on to grief, our loved ones are held back. We affect them with our pain. As difficult as it may be, to heal our loved ones and ourselves, we must release them and move forward. We can then become even closer to them because they are free and no longer bound to the confines of the earth. Their love for us will always continue.

Signs

If you imagine that you sense that I am near,
believe it to be true and do not fear.

If you see me in your dreams and you feel them to
be real, I am just paying you a visit, even though
it may seem surreal.

If you see the house lights begin to flicker or burn
out, it is just me. Please don't doubt.

If you smell an essence that reminds you of me,
breathe it in, close your eyes, and then let it be.

If you feel my presence, stop and look around; trust
this new perception that you have found.

If you hear a song that speaks to your heart
or makes you cry, know that it's me and I
am always close by.

If you look at the sky and see a rainbow or
a beautiful butterfly, it's me again just saying hi!

If you question my presence, believe in
each sign. I am doing great. I am just fine.

I am on my soul's journey in the spiritual
realm. I am never too far away to say that
I love you in every way.

Never doubt, be open and aware. It is me always
sharing how much I care.

Remember ~ I am always here!

I love getting signs from Adam. It is what keeps me going. What I enjoy most is helping people to be open and aware of the many signs that our loved ones show us. The following pages will explain some of the ways that Adam has made contact with me through the years. Signs are symbols and reassurances of loved ones' love for us. Perhaps you will recognize some of these subtleties or signs from your loved one.

FOUR

∞

Signs from Adam

Look for the subtleties—"I asked for a sign and the wind came through the window and knocked Adam's picture down."

Adam continues to show me signs daily, which have been substantial. Some of these signs are in the form of exact times on the clock that had special meaning for Adam and me. Specific numbers, electricity that suddenly sparked, or lights that suddenly turned off or would flicker and license plates with meaningful messages all have relevance. His favorite songs suddenly come on the radio when I think about him; hummingbirds or feathers; seeing his spirit in the corner of my eye and dimes that I have continued to find throughout the years all have relevance.

When I first moved to Southern California, I found a very reputable, intuitive tarot reader. My question was about Adam. The hummingbird card turned over, and she said, "This is your son! He stands for joy, prosperity, and abundance."

Many times, when I talk about Adam, a hummingbird will fly and dance before my eyes. Without a doubt, I know that this is Adam. Birds have always been special to Adam and me. We would imagine how astounding it would be to fly like a bird. Birds represent vision and freedom. I often see doves that perch on my fence and stay for long periods.

Feathers of all sizes have appeared right at my feet, and I have found them in places one would not normally find them. Feathers fall from the sky and land at my feet. There were times I found several feathers of various sizes in my house lying on the floor. People have given feathers to me and mentioned that they were from Adam.

Years ago, I started finding dimes everywhere and consistently. They were always tails up. I would be taking a walk and find them right in the middle of a path. It was happening to such an extent that I determined this to be a sign from Adam. Even my son Daniel began to find them as well. There were many times Daniel and I were together and looked down, and there would be a dime directly at our feet. We would reply by exclaiming, "There's Adam telling us hi."

I began to share these events with my family and friends. As soon as I shared my experience about finding dimes everywhere, they, too, began to find dimes tails up everywhere.

Numbers were, and continue to be, a big thing between Adam and me. His birthday was October 13. I began to look at the clock, and most frequently, it would read 10:13. I began to realize that this was no coincidence. It was Adam's birthday. Daniel also sees 10:13 on the clock recurrently.

I used to work in a restaurant, and every time I would clock in, the clock would register a relevant three-digit number sequence. It never failed. If it was a special occasion like a birthday or anniversary. I would ask Adam for a sign, and sure enough, it would read 111 or 420, a sequence that only meant something to Adam and me. The number sequences 11:11, 1:11, 4:20, or 10:13 all meant something prior to Adam's death, and I have always known that they were a sign from Adam.

Years before Adam died, we both noticed that everywhere we looked, we would see 11:11. This was revealed on digital clocks, receipts, or anything that had a numerical sequence. At that time, I did not realize what it meant—only that it must have been something of importance. Within a year of Adam's death, I was reading the book *The End Times: New Information for Personal Peace; Kryon, Book I* by Lee Carroll.[1] On the page I was reading appeared the significance of what the master number 11:11 means. I can still remember how astounded I felt at that moment. Kryon, the nonphysical entity channeled by Lee Carroll, states that it is a gateway or a wake-up call for light workers. A light worker is someone who makes an agreement on the spiritual plane to come to Earth to hold the light. His objective in this incarnation is to heal and to help raise the vibration of this planet. My belief is that when this number sequence occurs, an angel is tapping your shoulder to look at the clock to remind you to hold the energy and vibration for world peace and love. Many others acknowledge 11:11 and believe in this explanation.

Adam's purpose on this physical plane and beyond has been amazing. I know that it was planned before we came here for the two of us to work together in this incarnation. I felt his powerful presence and energy while I was pregnant with him. In retrospect, it was a very intense and sacred feeling. I had lost a baby about three years prior to becoming pregnant with Adam. I always had a strong feeling that Adam was reincarnated as the same soul. It was obvious that this soul had a profound calling.

When Adam was sixteen years old, he asked me if I knew what 420 meant. I said that I did not. He told me that it was a police code. This code was established when the police arrested someone for smoking marijuana. As most things do, it managed to become publicly known. Therefore April 20 (420) became known as national smoke-out day. After he shared that little gem of information with me, we shared a good laugh. Since that time, I have been seeing the number 420 for years on clocks, license plates, and even carved into tables. Every time I see 420, which is often, I believe it is Adam telling me to laugh, to lighten up, and not to take anything too seriously.

The license plate is a very common way for your loved one to give you a message. I have received many signs throughout the years. A sign can be in the form of numbers, such as 420 or 111, or letters that mean something just to the two of you. Dragonflies and white butterflies are other symbols that remind me of Adam. They represent spirituality to me. I have had nature's messengers fly right up to me and circle me just to deliver a hello from Adam and to let me know he is around. Whenever I feel it is Adam, I believe it is.

I would be in a store and I would be thinking about Adam or perhaps talking about him. Suddenly, someone would announce over the loudspeaker the name *Adam*. At first, I would be amazed at the many ways that Adam would make contact with me, but now it is so natural that I expect it.

On his birthday one year, I said out loud, "Adam, give me a sign if you are here." Within minutes, the wind came through the window and blew his picture down on the floor. It did not break. I acknowledged the sign by saying, "Thanks, Adam."

Oftentimes, I would be driving in my car thinking of him, and a song would come on that he used to love. I would feel happy and sad, and then I would begin to cry. My emotions are so strongly connected to him.

I believe that Adam helped manifest the house we bought when we were looking to move to California. We had flown in from Michigan and looked at more than twenty-five houses in a three-day period, and none of them worked out. The kids and I were returning to Michigan in the morning without any luck. We were very disappointed. I then said a silent prayer and asked Adam for help. The realtor said, "Let's go back to the office to check one more time." When we got back to the office, there were two more homes to look at. The last one was the best one that we had seen during the whole three-day excursion. We bought this home and live in it to this day. It has a beautiful view of the ocean and valley as well as a beautiful sunset every day of the year. Adam and I have always loved sunsets and used to share them on a regular basis. It was another way for Adam to look out for our family and me. Ironically, the day Adam fell to his death, he was climbing to reach the top of the mountain with his friends to watch the sun set over Lake Tahoe.

As I wrote this page, it was no surprise that the digital clock next to my desk had a digital date on it. The date read November 11, or 11/11. I went upstairs later to see Daniel. Daniel said, "Mom, look at the clock!" The time was 10:13: Adam's birthday.

I have felt Adam brush against my face with such a soft touch. It felt like he was kissing my cheek. I often see his spirit out of the corner of my eye. When I look back, he disappears.

Candles are also an important ritual and sign to me. I have them lit all the time in my home. There are times that I am just staring at the flame, and it will begin to flicker very bright and large. I ask, "Adam, is that you?" The flame will begin to dance. Candles are another way that Spirit communicates.

After reading a book on life-after-death communication, someone had an experience with his deceased loved one in a dream. He had a telephone conversation with his loved one. I thought that this was fascinating. I decided to ask Adam to call me. To my surprise, it was that same night. In my dream, the phone rang, and Adam's voice was on the line. I said hello, and Adam replied, "Hi, Mom. It's me."

I still remember saying, "Adam, Adam, is that you?"

He replied, "Yes. I just want you to know I love you and I am fine." I said, "Adam, are you there?" There was no reply. Our wonderful but brief conversation was over. It was so inspiring that I was able to hear his voice so loud and clear. I was in awe.

Three years ago, Adam started appearing as a white tiger. I saw white tigers everywhere. Even my friends started seeing them. Next thing I knew, one of my friends, Vicki, came to our mediumship class and gave me a baby white stuffed tiger that she had won. She said she immediately thought of me. My other friend, Lisa, gave me a baby white tiger puzzle that she purchased. Adam also began manifesting white tigers to my teacher, Diana, who is a medium. It was quite comical. It was a symbol that Adam wanted us to recognize for whatever it meant to him.

Electricity is a common sign. Within three months after Adam passed away, the lightbulbs in the kitchen began to flicker and would often burn out. I would replace the burned out ones, and within a few days, they would flicker and burn out again. We had lived in our home for six years, and this had never occurred before. Adam's communication from the other side never gets old.

I cherish these moments. His communication with me still places me in a state of amazement. Most people with whom I have had conversations whose loved ones have passed over have experienced signs from them. They have shared with me how wonderful it made them feel to know that their loved ones, who were in Spirit, were communicating with them.

Spirits will attend their own funerals and show up at the burial service. This is very common. The people that are open to Spirit are the ones who will see them, hear them, smell them, and feel them. Oftentimes, they will show up as a white butterfly flying around the casket or something else that you may recognize that has relevance to you, and other times, you will see a white mist forming above the casket. I have even heard of a bright, colorful rainbow glistening across the sky.

Just notice the signs, no matter how subtle they may be. They are heaven-sent. Our loved ones and angels drop feathers, coins, and other signs in our paths to remind us that we are loved and that we are never alone. I never realized how close I was to the other side until Adam died. It has become very natural to me to communicate with Adam, and numerous other spirits as well.

I was pregnant with Adam when my grandfather died. I was devastated because I was very close to my grandpa. I would dream about him often, and he would come to me in my dreams to tell me how much he loved me. I still remember these dreams so vividly. It was not until Adam died that I realized that my grandpa was actually visiting me. We were communicating between the two worlds.

My hope is that anyone who has not yet received a sign will receive one. Ask for one and be open to it. Be aware. It may be something that only you and your child or loved one will recognize. It makes those who are in Spirit very happy when we recognize that these very special signs are from them.

Since my son's death, my journey continues to be ever expanding. I am eternally grateful for this evolution in my growth. It is my goal to express my love, to give hope, to assist others in the healing process, and to offer service to my fellow human beings. There is so much more than this life on Earth. Our loved ones want to show us the journey that we are on and the learning that we must continue on both sides of the veil. The most important thing that they want us to know is *Love Is Eternal and Never Dies*.

Note

1.   Lee Caroll, *The End Times: New Information for Personal Peace; Kryon, Book I* (Del Mar, CA: Kryon Writers, 1993).

FIVE

∞

Unconditional Love

"I miss him deeply, but he often lets me know that he is fine and that our love is unconditional."

The last time I saw Adam, I was in my dad's car. I was in the passenger seat. My dad was driving, and both Adam and Daniel were in the backseat. We were dropping Adam off at his friend's house. Just before the car stopped, Adam wrapped his arms around me and the seat, squeezed me tightly with such intensity, and said, "I love you, Mom."

I looked back at him, and I remember thinking that his love was so strong, it flowed right through me. I turned around and grabbed his head, pulled it toward me, and kissed him on the forehead. I can still smell him and taste his salty skin. Then Adam kissed Daniel good-bye and told him that he loved him, too, and climbed out of the car. Adam looked back at my dad and said, "I love you, Grandpa. Peace!"

Prior to this time, Adam and his grandpa were not speaking to one another. I looked at my dad and asked him, "Did you hear that?" He said that he did. It was a miracle. I got out of the car, and Adam and I hugged, kissed, and said I love you one last time. I got back into the car, looked out the window, and watched him walk down the street with his long blonde hair and his baggy jeans. This was the last time I saw Adam alive. It is etched permanently in my mind forever. It was such a powerful moment.

My son Adam was spiritual, compassionate, and kind. He came to teach and experience unconditional love. He was the teacher, student, and my son. His primary purpose in this life was unselfishly to give his heart and soul. He always cared for the underdog, regardless of whatever or wherever the situation was. From a very young age to the day that Adam died, he always stood up for the less fortunate child, the one who could not stand up for himself or herself. That child became Adam's friend, and it made Adam feel good that he was able to help someone. If he was protecting someone from a fight, standing up for a friend, or feeding a homeless person, it did not matter. He was always there.

From the beginning, Adam was a very wise person with the maturity of a man, with a huge heart in a boy's body, who was shy, sensitive, and intuitive. My older brother John nicknamed him "Little Man." All of Adam's friends constantly validated these traits and his importance to them. These values seemed so natural for him. Yet he was amused when he heard what was said about him after he parted. Yes, Adam was special—not because he was mine, but because his gifts to give and to love unconditionally were ahead of his time.

As Adam grew older, he shared his words of wisdom, peace, and love with many friends. As a result, he changed many lives with his highly developed spiritual beliefs. Adam was a highly sensitive and deep child. It would not take much for him to get his feelings hurt and cry. If someone did not treat him right, he could not understand. I would let him know how special and strong he was and tell him to rise above the situation. I would discuss with him forgiveness, the laws of the universe, and Karma (the laws of attraction or, simply put, what goes around comes around). He did not hold dear anyone who did not show him respect. He knew that respect was an essential ingredient to love.

Adam loved nature. He was one with the earth. He understood the immutable laws of the universe. He also understood the importance of respecting the earth. He innately knew that we are all connected and that everything is about love.

Adam was devoid of fear. He was like an eagle living from moment to moment and unafraid of anything, flying from one mountaintop to another. He was a fully developed soul who believed in independence and the importance of freedom. He also believed that you could not take life for granted because it goes by so quickly. Adam lived his life full of adventure, love, compassion, laughter, and joy. These were the standards that he believed in and cherished in his short life.

Adam experienced life rather quickly—always wanting to be free, the free spirit he was destined to be. He died instantly that day, without any pain. It was his time to go. Even though my son is on the other side of the veil, he continues to work through me to share with the world that unconditional love is the only thing that is real. I miss him deeply. When he died, it was though time stopped. When our communication to each other became apparent, I made a choice to seek the greater truths once again. I have been on the Journey of Expansion ever since. We are all connected and one with the Divine. He also lets me know that when it is my time to go, he will be awaiting my arrival, embraced in the white light and our Eternal Love.

This has been a very personal journey from the loss of a son to Eternal Love. I will forever cherish his life. I hope that you who read my experiences will receive the same comfort and healing that comes with knowing that *Love Is Eternal and Never Dies.*

Self-Expressions

Self-Expressions

Self-Expressions

Self-Expressions

Praise for Loretta?s Line of Empathy Greeting Cards

Your wonderful poem "Celebrate" meant so much to me. I lost my husband and best friend of fifty-two years. I had nothing to look forward to; the love of my life was gone. Then my granddaughter Misty sent me a card with your poem on it. You reminded me that I was not alone. I read your poem daily. Your card came to me when I needed it most. Thank you, Loretta. I know my husband is near.

DP, WA.

The sentimental cards created by Loretta are warm, caring, and straight from the heart. She wrote the perfect verse so that I could express my feelings to a family member after the loss of our parents. The card I sent was called "Celebrate," and I could not have said it better myself!

LH, CA.

Loretta's words are a true gift. Her words allow us to feel connected with the one who has passed. I have never seen cards that are such a gift—a gift of seeing God's true light and meaning. . . . I was able to send the card "Released" to a friend whose husband died from a four-year battle with cancer. She has the card up in her room as a reminder that there are never any good-byes and life is not over when you die. She broke down in tears, saying that her husband used to say that exact phrase. Thank you, Loretta, for the powerful words that transcend us toward peace as well as help us *let go!*

CS, CA.

Through the years, I have read, sent, and received many different cards. Some were nice, some unique, some inspiring. However, I cannot remember being moved by any of them the way Loretta's cards moved me when I first read them. The connection was so real; it was almost as though I was sent on an emotional journey as I was reading them. Though the theme of Loretta's cards is about being comforted after losing a loved one, I actually gave one of her cards as a birthday card. I guess a birthday is a good occasion to be reminded of how precious a gift life is.

MJ, CA.

I purchased two of Loretta's beautiful cards for a few of my friends whose fathers and mothers passed away. They called me right away to say how beautiful and thoughtful the cards were. . . . I strongly recommend her inspirational cards and poetry to anyone who is going through trauma or a death in the family.

AS, CA.